AGES

Just Puzzling!

Mazes & Dot-to-Dots

Your first stop for fun and learning!

Brighter Child®
An imprint of Carson-Dellosa Publishing LLC
Greensboro, North Carolina

Brighter Child®
An imprint of Carson-Dellosa Publishing LLC
P.O. Box 35665
Greensboro, NC 27425 USA

Printed in the USA • All rights reserved.   ISBN 978-1-60996-976-9

01-086121151

Table of Contents

Mazes

Dot-to-Dots

Digging Up Bones

Directions: Help the scientist find the dinosaur bones. Then, color the picture.

The Lost Nest

Directions: Help the dinosaur mother find her nest of eggs. Then, color the picture.

A Very Worried Dinosaur

Directions: Help the dinosaur find its baby. Then, color the picture.

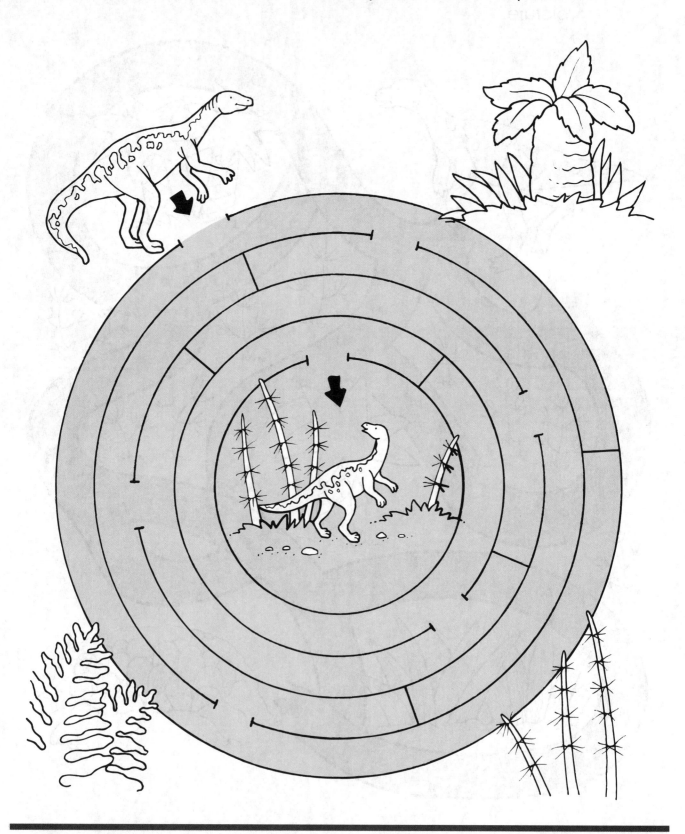

Fun on Skis

Directions: Help the skier down the mountain. Then, color the picture.

A Space Trip

Directions: Find the way to the moon. Then, color the picture.

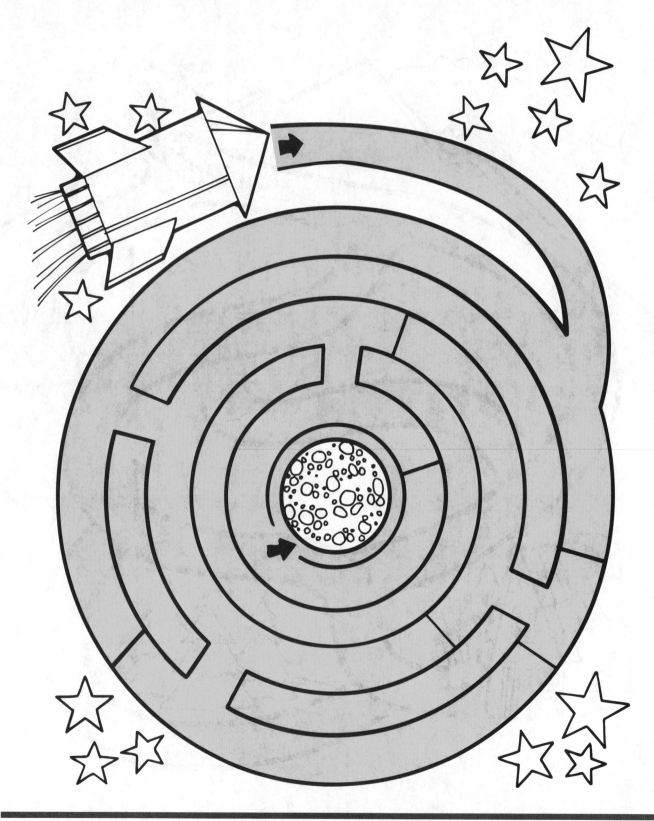

A Lost Mitten

Directions: Help the girl find her mitten. Then, color the picture.

A Garden Helper

Directions: Find the way to the flower garden. Then, color the picture.

A Boat Ride

Directions: Follow the path to the island. Then, color the picture.

Forest Babies

Directions: Help the babies find their mothers. Then, color the picture.

Pinky's Bedtime

Directions: Find the way to Pinky's bed. Then, color the picture.

Time for Art

Directions: Help Anna find her drawing pad. Then, color the picture.

Soccer Fun

Directions: Help the soccer player score a goal. Then, color the picture.

Bath Time

Directions: Help the boy get to the bathtub. Then, color the picture.

Bubble Gum

Directions: Help the girl find the gum. Then, color the picture.

A Lost Shoe

Directions: Help the bug find its shoe. Then, color the picture.

Time for Bed

Directions: Help the sleepy bear find the bed. Then, color the picture.

Busy Beaver

Directions: Help the beaver find the water. Then, color the picture.

Springtime

Directions: Help the bunny find the egg. Then, color the picture.

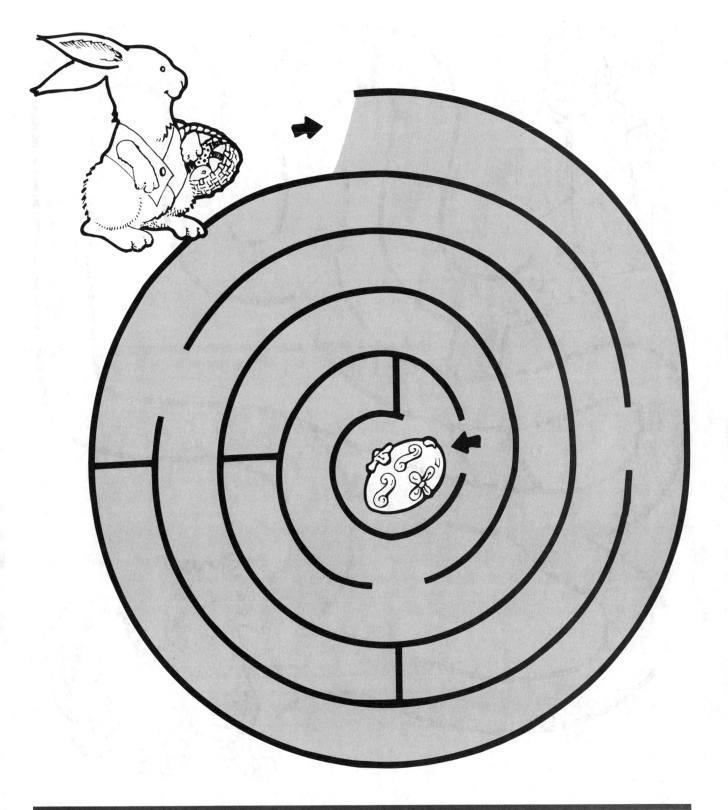

Find the Dragon

Directions: Help the knight find the dragon. Then, color the picture.

Making Honey

Directions: Help the bee find the hive. Then, color the picture.

Where Is It?

Directions: Help the screwdriver find the screw. Then, color the picture.

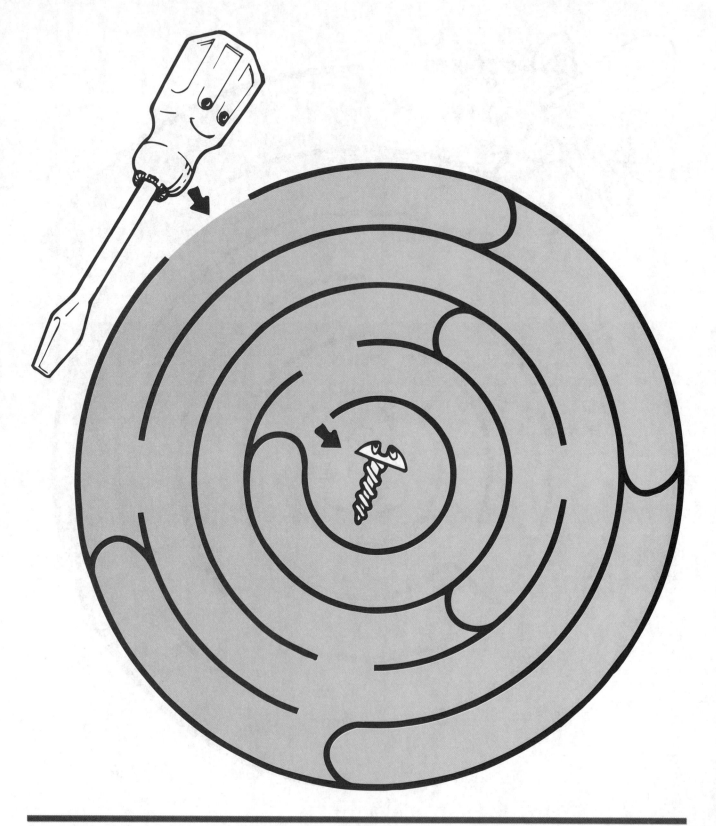

Beeline to Spring

Directions: Help the honeybee find the apple blossom. Then, color the picture.

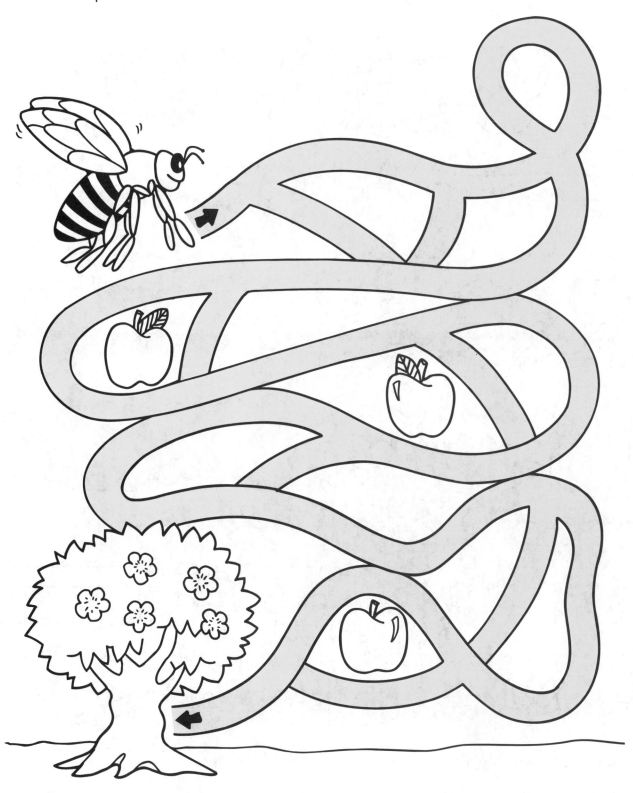

Hopping Down the Bunny Trail

Directions: Help the rabbit find the carrot patch. Then, color the picture.

Time for a Scrub!

Directions: Help the robin find the birdbath. Then, color the picture.

Fly Away Home

Directions: Help the butterfly find the flower garden. Then, color the picture.

Hungry Crows

Directions: Help the crows find the corn field. Then, color the picture.

Home Sweet Home

Directions: Help the Pilgrim girl and boy find their home. Then, color the picture.

Little Lost Lamb

Directions: Help the lamb find its mother. Then, color the picture.

Let's Get to Work

Directions: Help the driver find the dump truck. Then, color the picture.

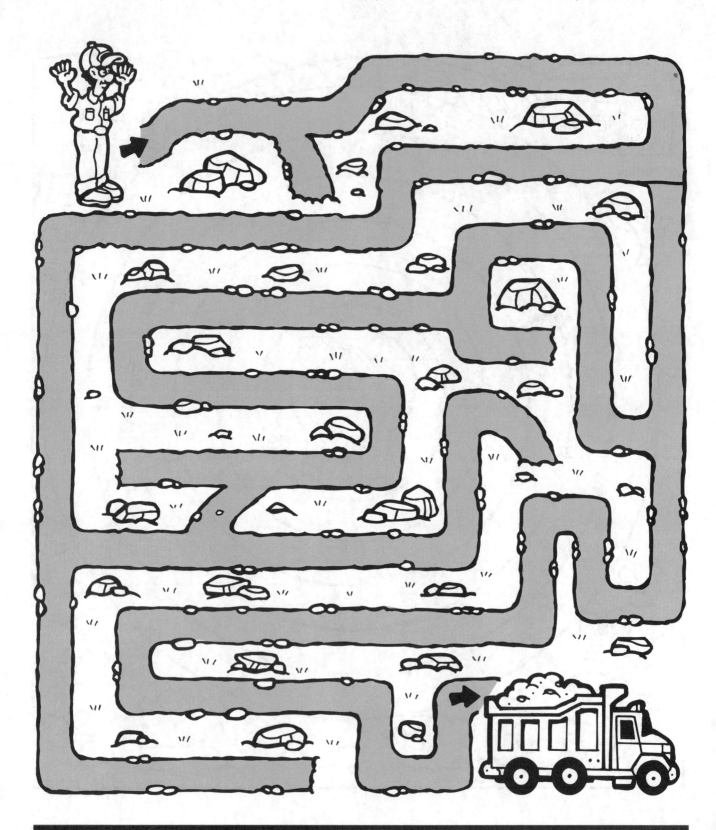

The New World

Directions: Help the Pilgrims find Plymouth Rock. Then, color the picture.

Digging a Hole

Directions: Help the backhoe find the dump truck. Then, color the picture.

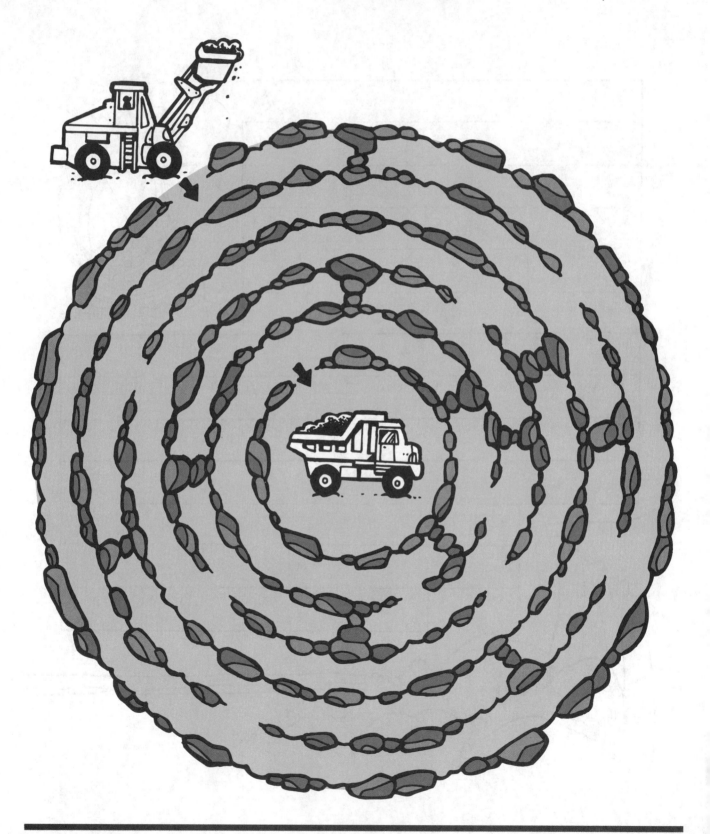

Time for a Break

Directions: Help the foreman find the lunch truck. Then, color the picture.

Back from the Fire

Directions: Help the fire engine get to the fire station. Then, color the picture.

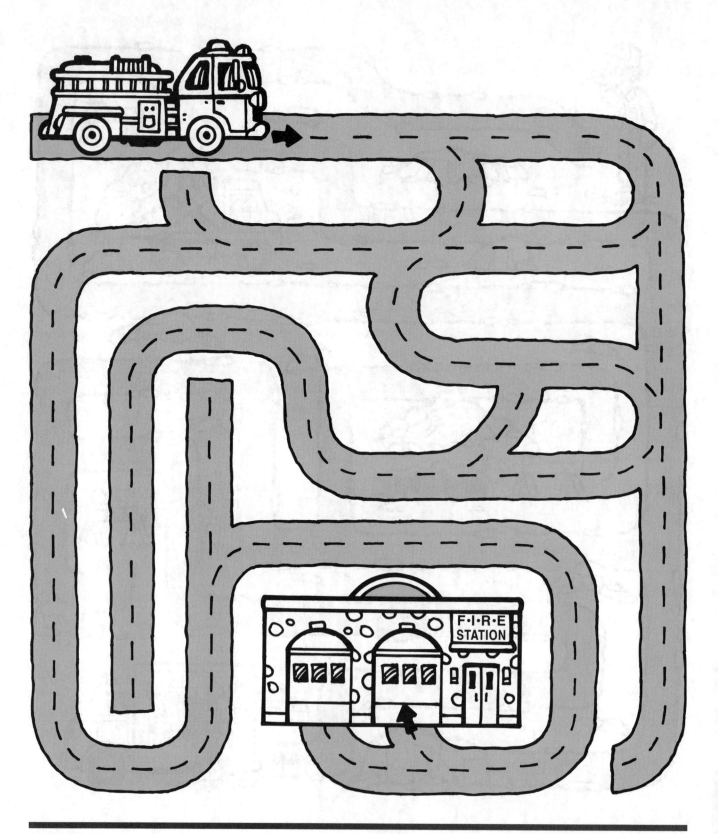

A Four-Alarm Maze

Directions: Help the firefighter get to the fire. Then, color the picture.

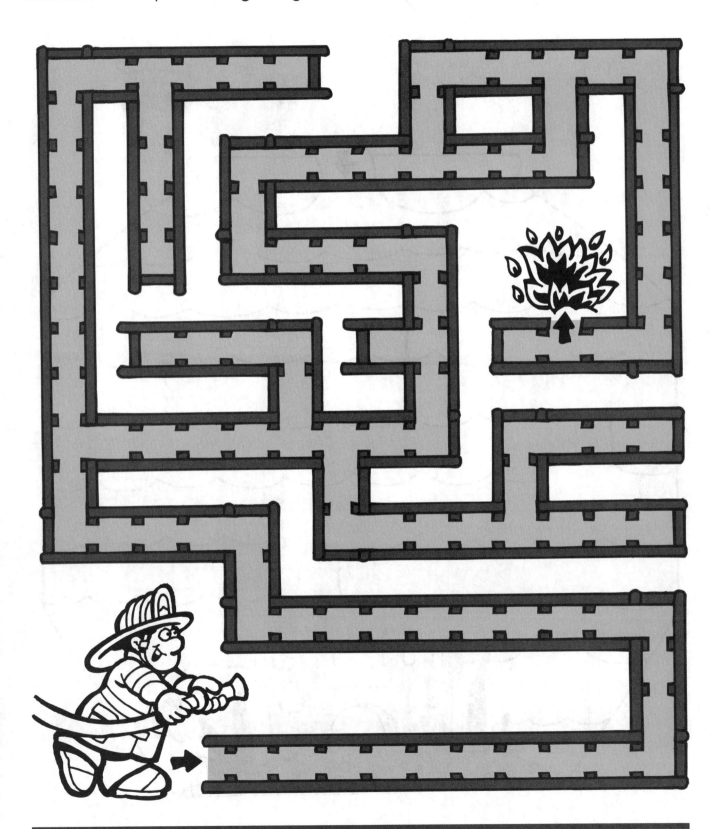

Castle Swim

Directions: Show the fish how to swim to the castle.

Keep the Beat

Directions: Connect the dots from **a** to **g**. Then, color to finish the picture.

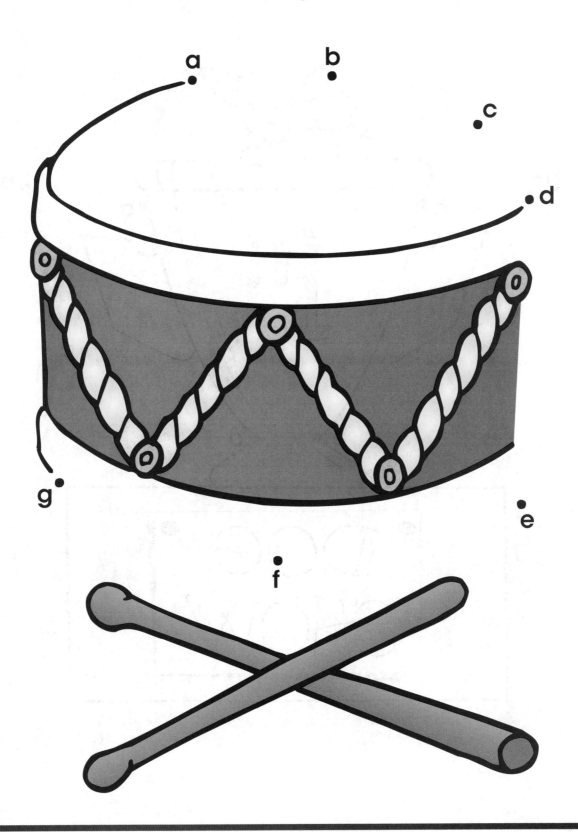

Chihuahua

Directions: Connect the dots from **a** to **h**. Then, color to finish the picture.

Sharing Time

Directions: Connect the dots from **A** to **J**. Then, color to finish the picture.

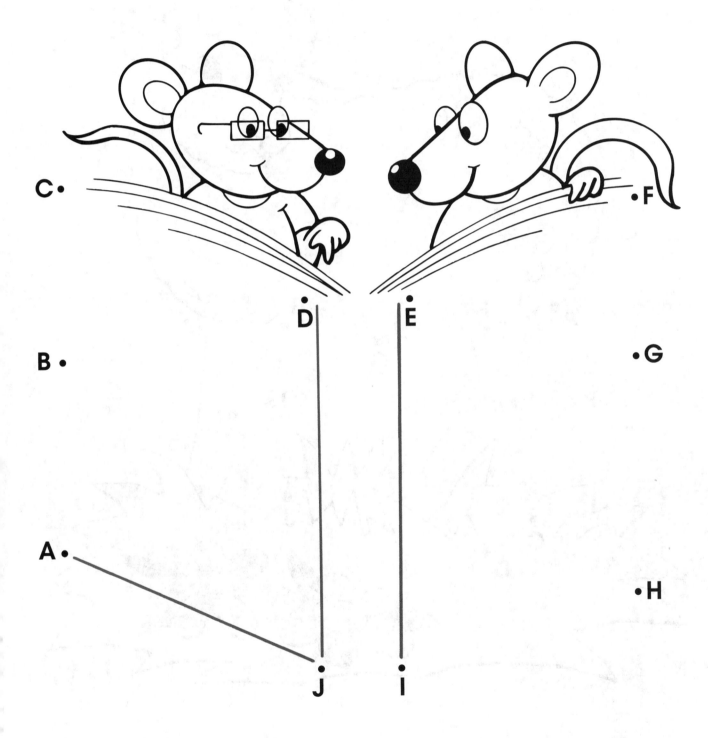

Lamb

Directions: Connect the dots from **A** to **M**. Then, color to finish the picture.

Sailing Away

Directions: Connect the dots from **A** to **M**. Then, color to finish the picture.

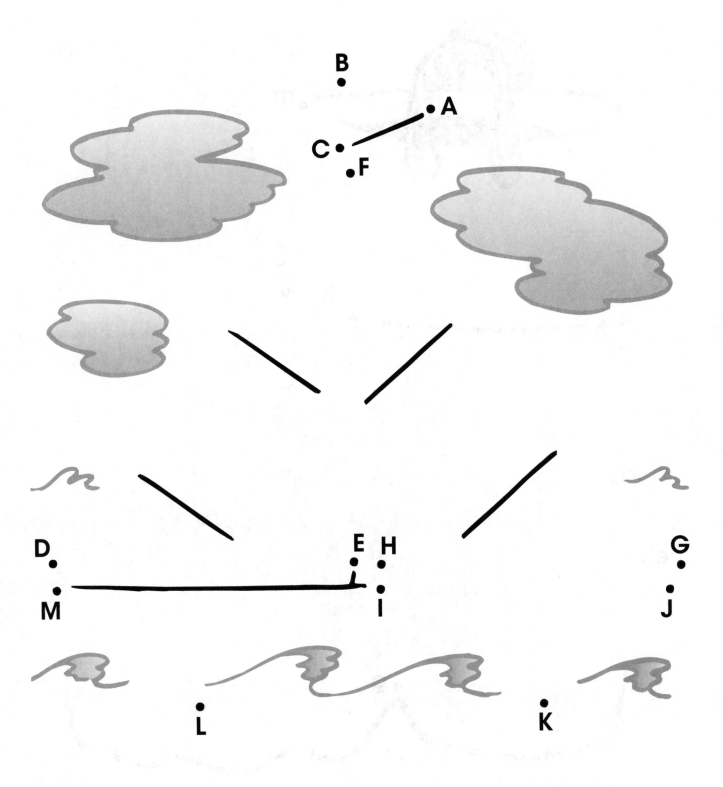

A Step in the Right Direction

Directions: Connect the dots from **a** to **m**. Then, color to finish the picture.

a•   •m

b•   •l
c•   •k

d•   •j

e•   •i

f•   •g   •h

Cockatoo

Directions: Connect the dots from **a** to **t**. Then, color to finish the picture.

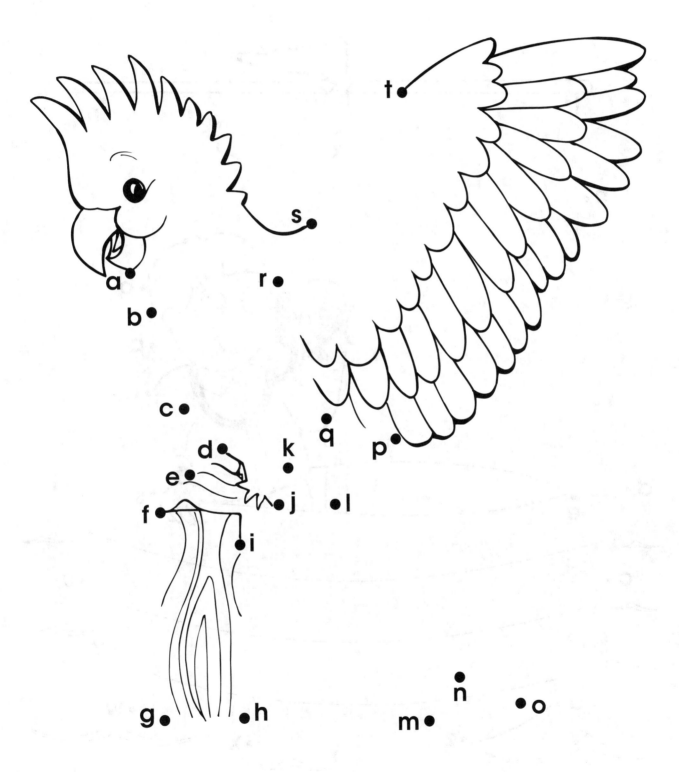

Let's Explore

Directions: Connect the dots from **a** to **z**. Then, color to finish the picture.

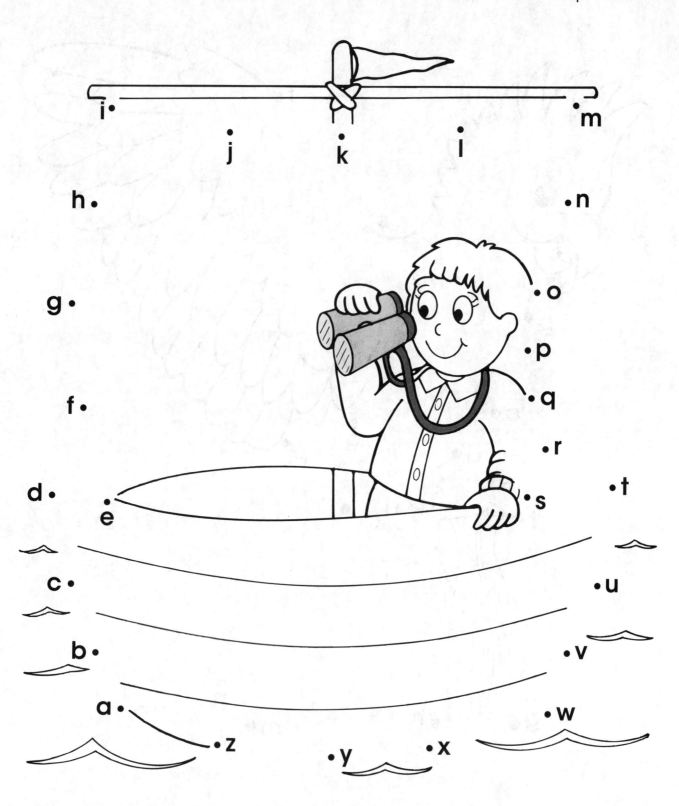

Friends for Life

Directions: Connect the dots from **A** to **Z**. Then, color to finish the picture.

Ready for Action

Directions: Connect the dots from **a** to **z**. Then, color to finish the picture.

On the Road

Directions: Connect the dots from **a** to **z**. Then, color to finish the picture.

To the Rescue

Directions: Connect the dots from **A** to **Z**. Then, color to finish the picture.

The Happy Scarecrow

Directions: Connect the dots from **A** to **Z**. Then, color to finish the picture.

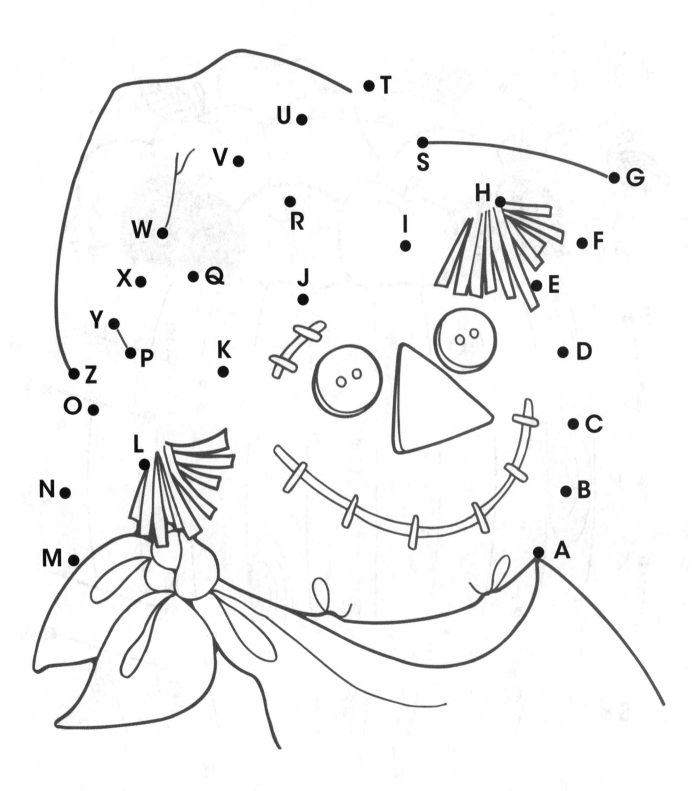

Full of Apples

Directions: Connect the dots from **A** to **Z**. Then, color to finish the picture.

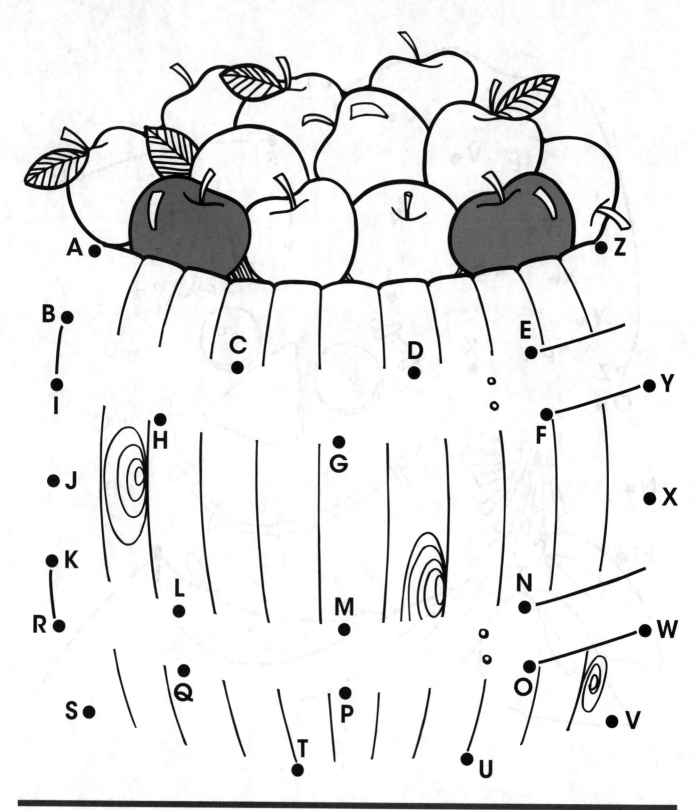

A Real Angel

Directions: Connect the dots from **A** to **Z**. Then, color to finish the picture.

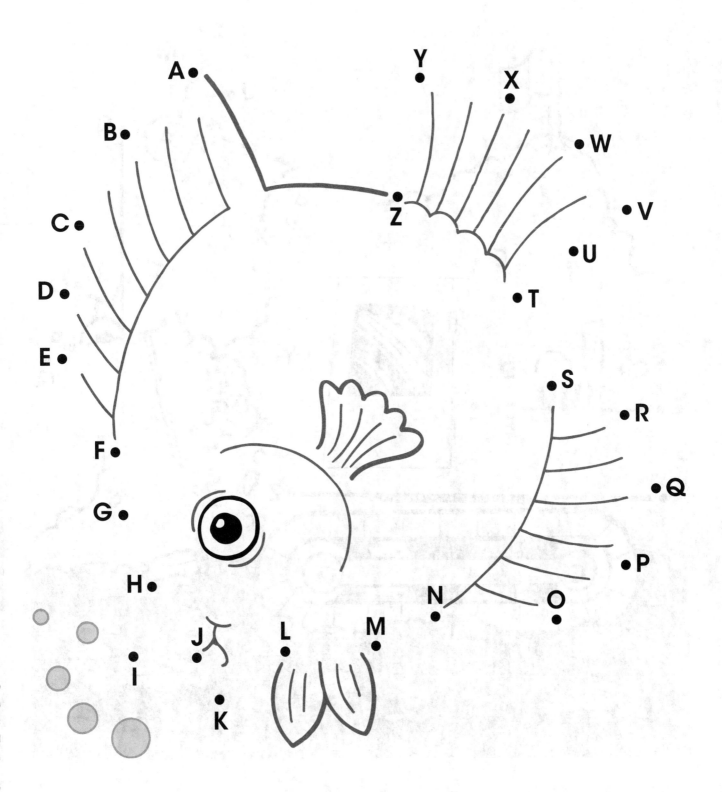

Digging Deep

Directions: Connect the dots from **A** to **Z**. Then, color to finish the picture.

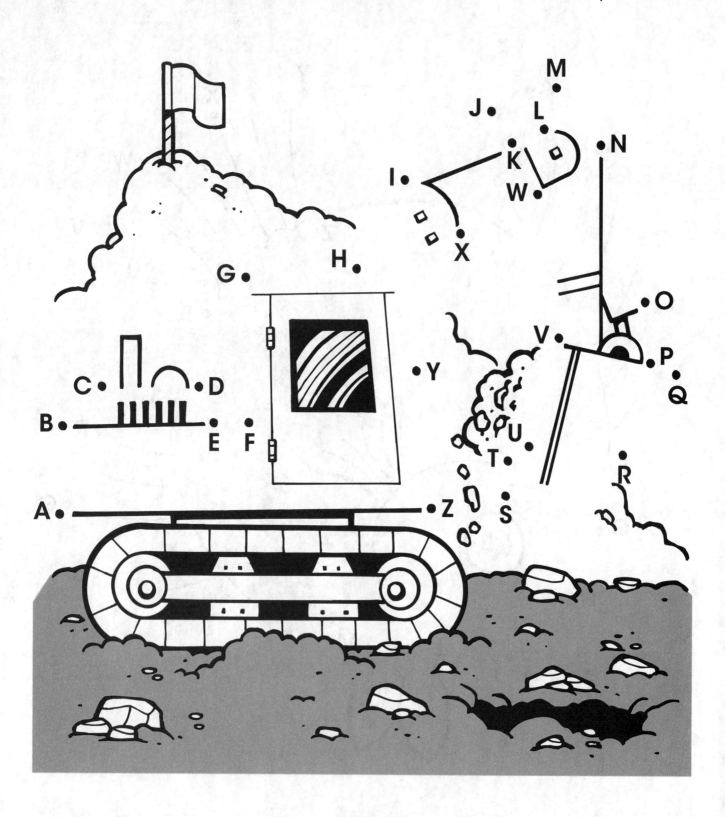

Sailing High

Directions: Connect the dots from **1** to **5**. Then, color to finish the picture.

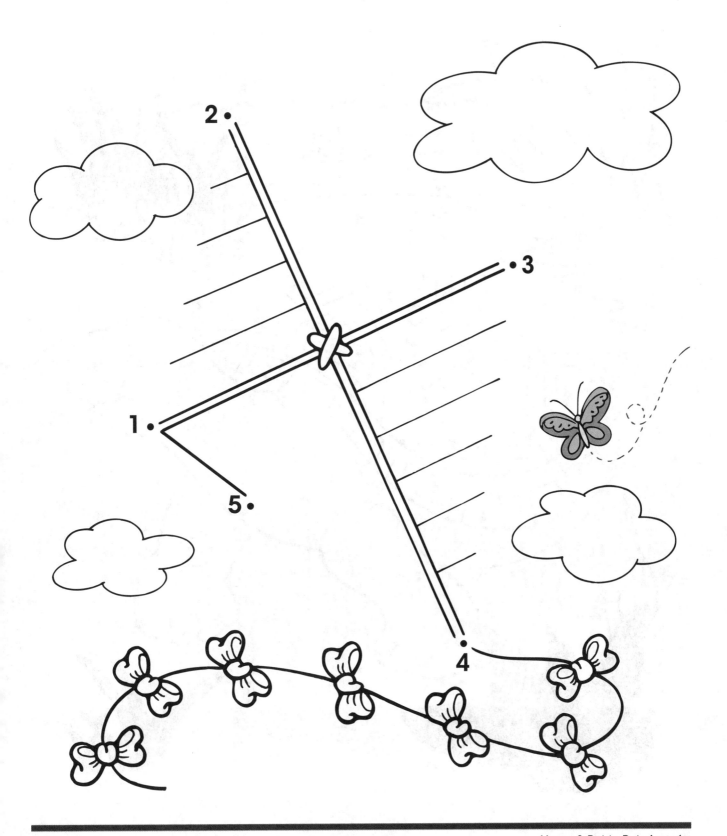

Tommy Tortoise

Directions: Connect the dots from **1** to **5**. Then, color to finish the picture.

Antonio Angelfish

Directions: Connect the dots from **1** to **10**. Then, color to finish the picture.

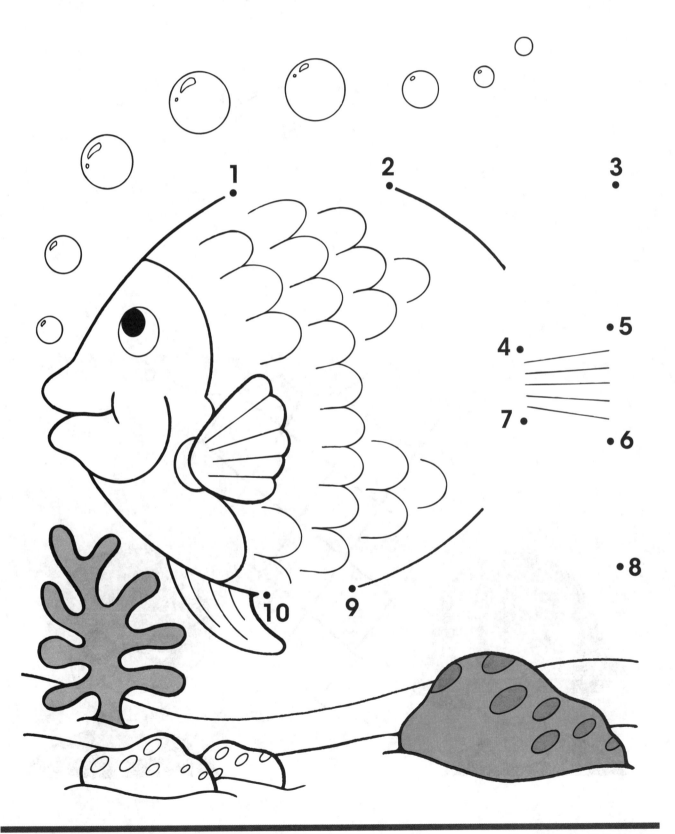

Cool and Sweet to Eat

Directions: Connect the dots from **1** to **8**. Then, color to finish the picture.

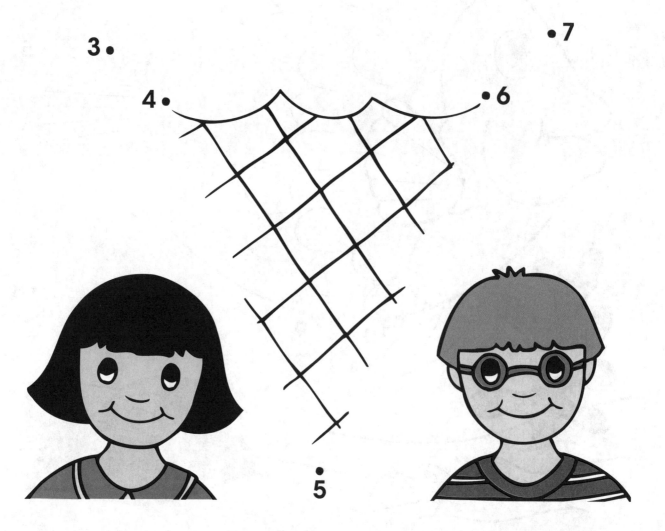

Perry Peacock

Directions: Connect the dots from **1** to **10**. Then, color to finish the picture.

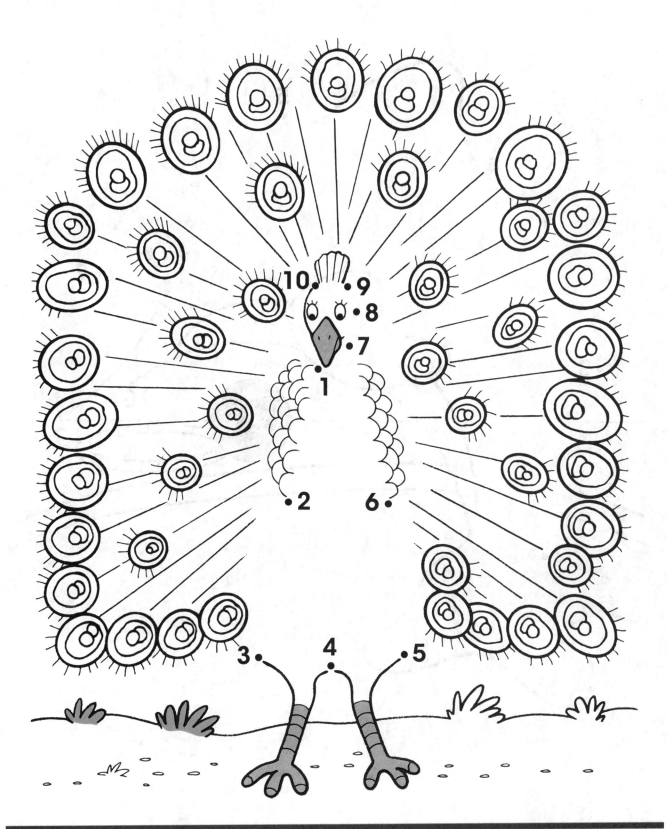

Derrick Dolphin

Directions: Connect the dots from **1** to **10**. Then, color to finish the picture.

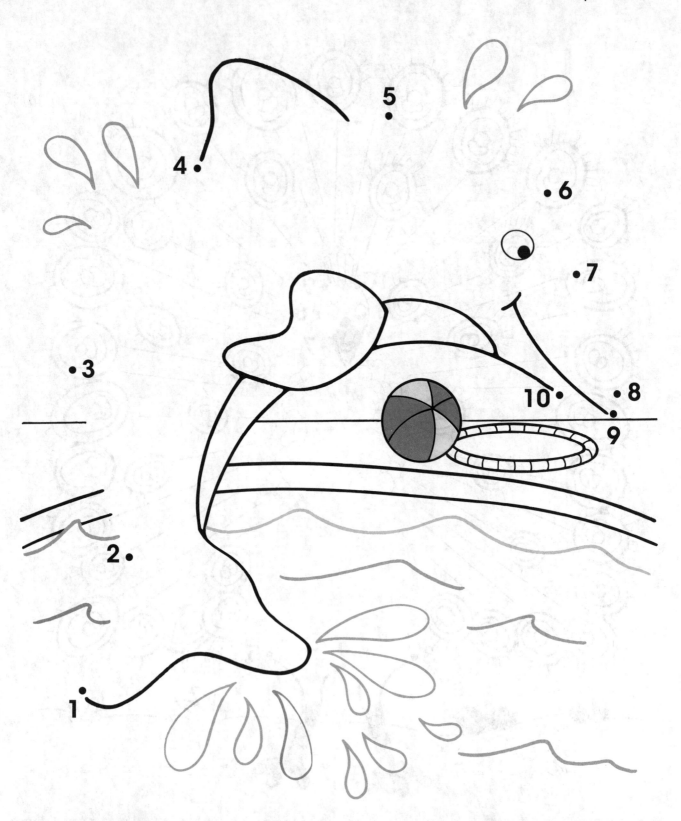

Suzanna Snake

Directions: Connect the dots from **1** to **10**. Then, color to finish the picture.

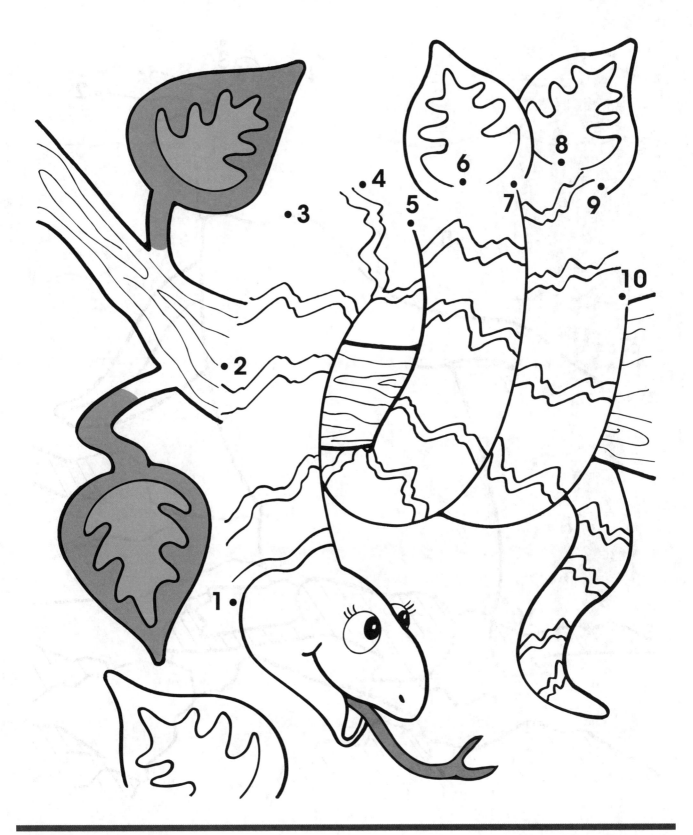

Peter Penguin

Directions: Connect the dots from **1** to **10**. Then, color to finish the picture.

Not a Dragon

Directions: Connect the dots from **1** to **12**. Then, color to finish the picture.

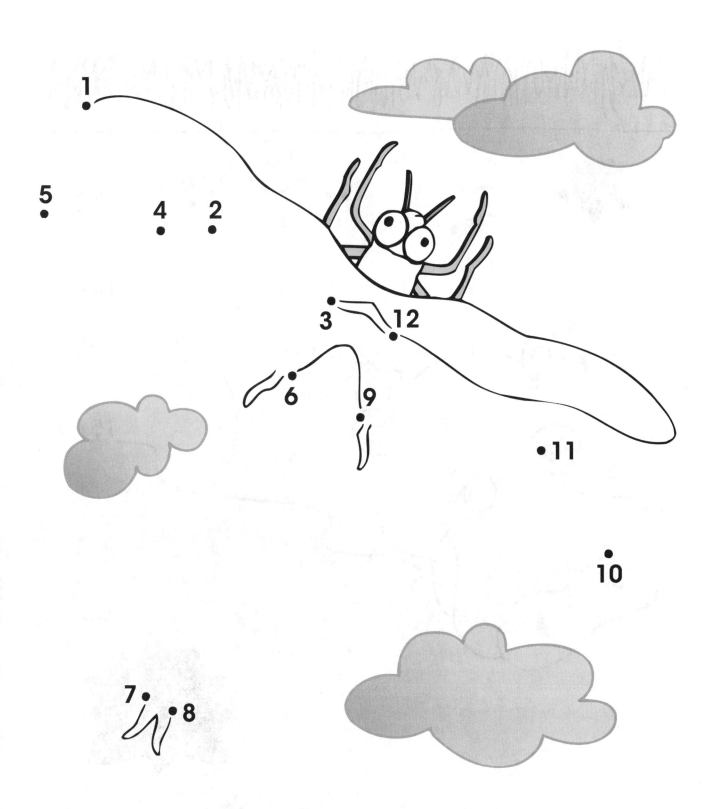

José Hippopotamus

Directions: Connect the dots from **1** to **15**. Then, color to finish the picture.

Luke Llama

Directions: Connect the dots from **1** to **15**. Then, color to finish the picture.

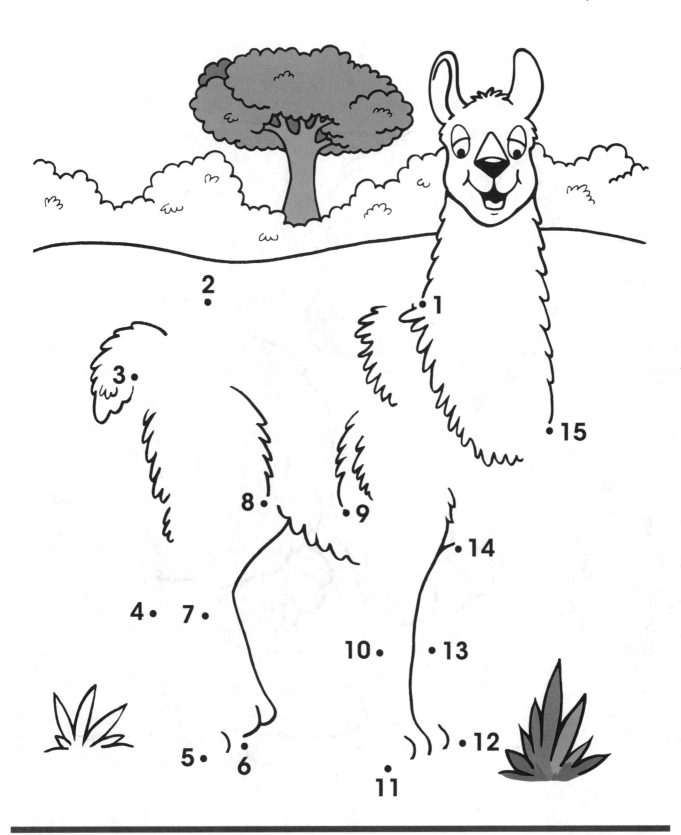

Pancho Polar Bear

Directions: Connect the dots from **1** to **15**. Then, color to finish the picture.

The Masked Hero

Directions: Connect the dots from **1** to **15**. Then, color to finish the picture.

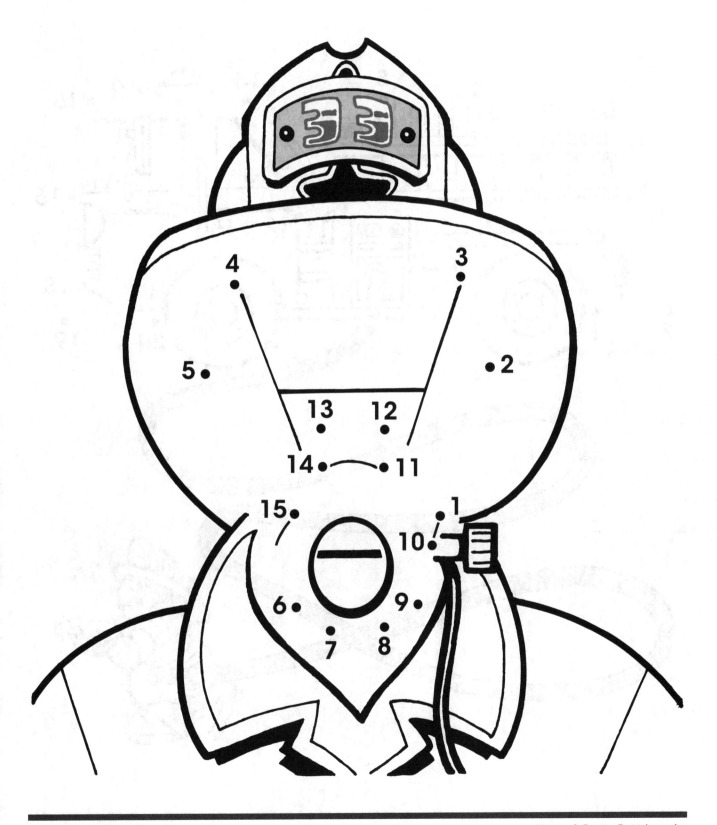

Fire Truck, Fire Truck

Directions: Connect the dots from **1** to **20**. Then, color to finish the picture.

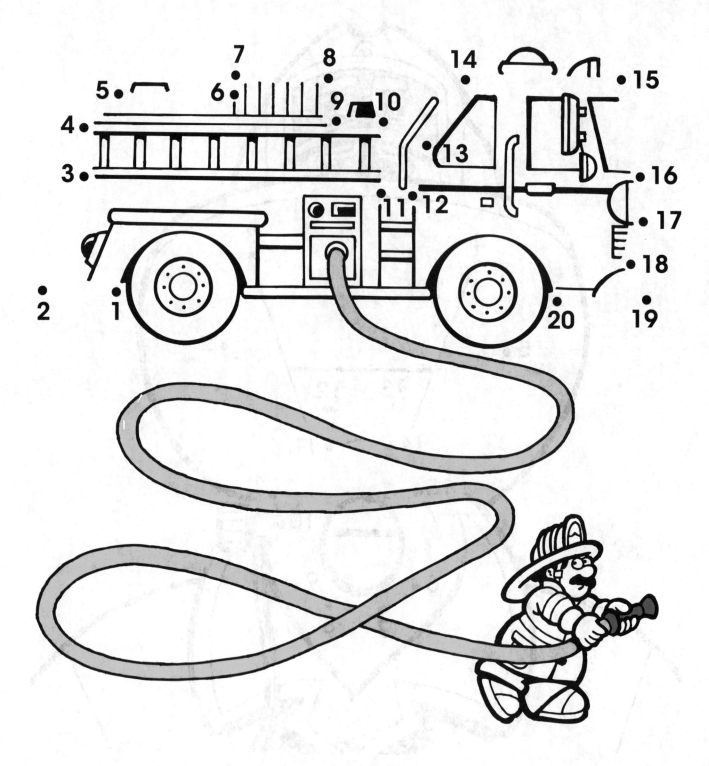

Carrying Cargo

Directions: Connect the dots from **1** to **20**. Then, color to finish the picture.

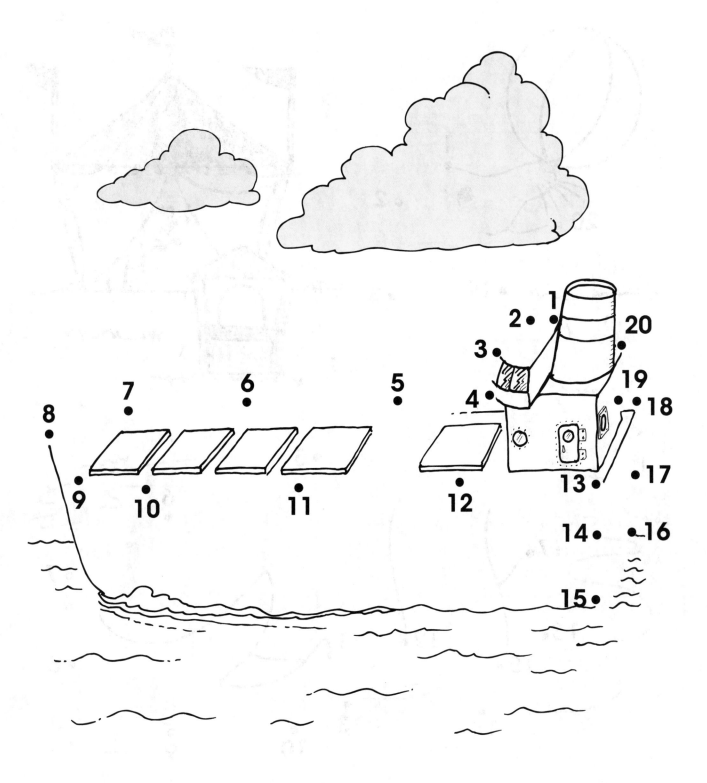

Balancing Trick

Directions: Connect the dots from **1** to **20**. Then, color to finish the picture.

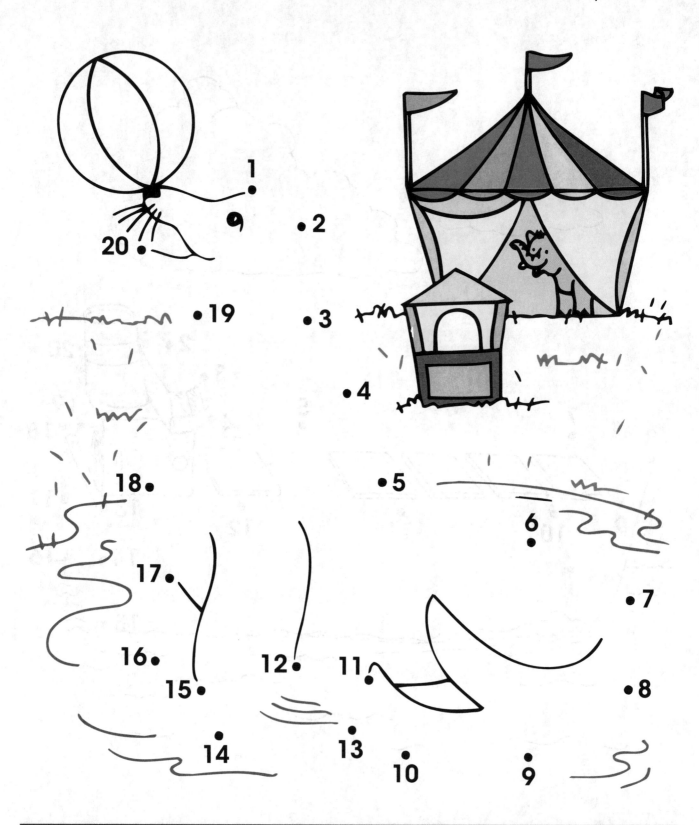

Philip Flamingo

Directions: Connect the dots from **1** to **20**. Then, color to finish the picture.

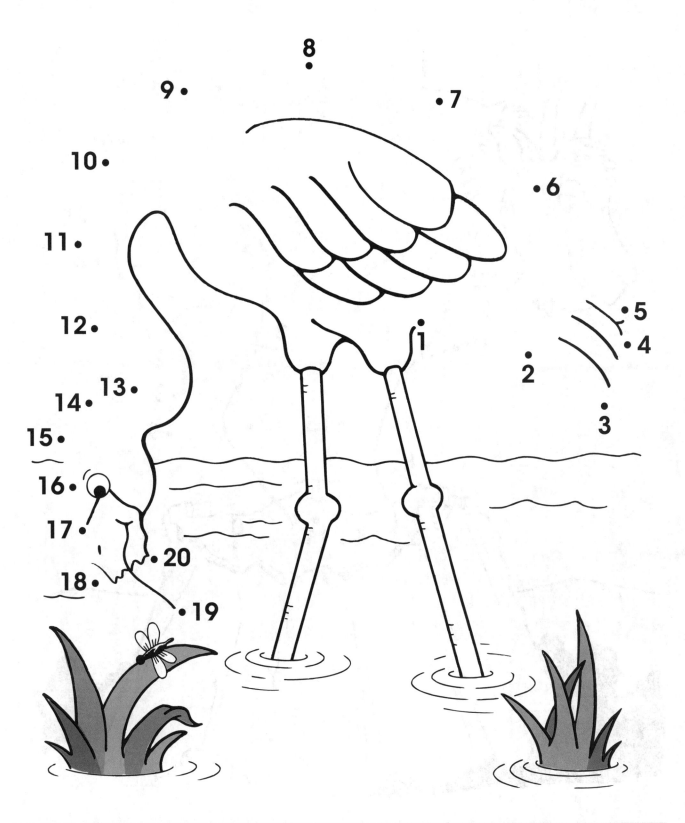

Mia Mountain Goat

Directions: Connect the dots from **1** to **20**. Then, color to finish the picture.

Andy Antelope

Directions: Color the dots from **1** to **25**. Then, color to finish the picture.

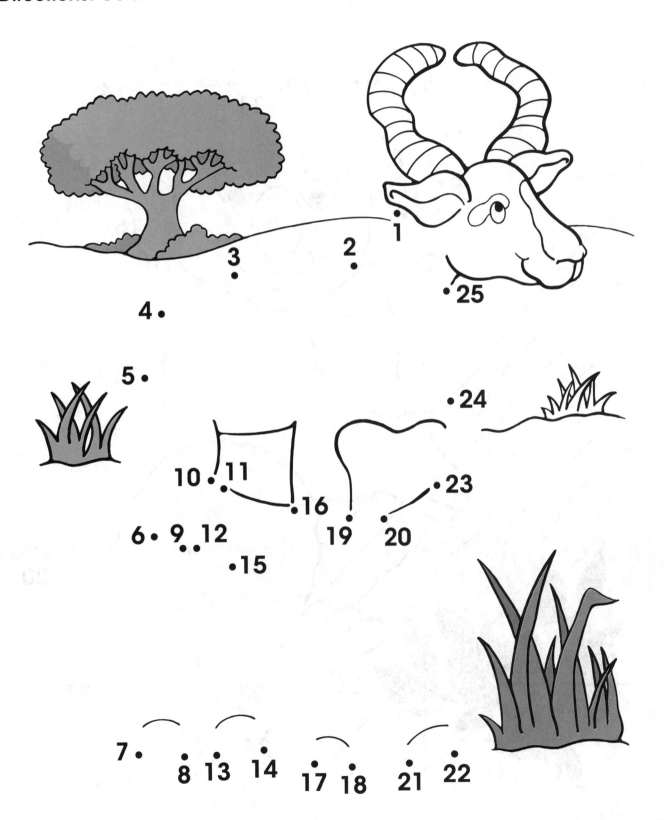

Kerin Koala

Directions: Connect the dots from **1** to **25**. Then, color to finish the picture.

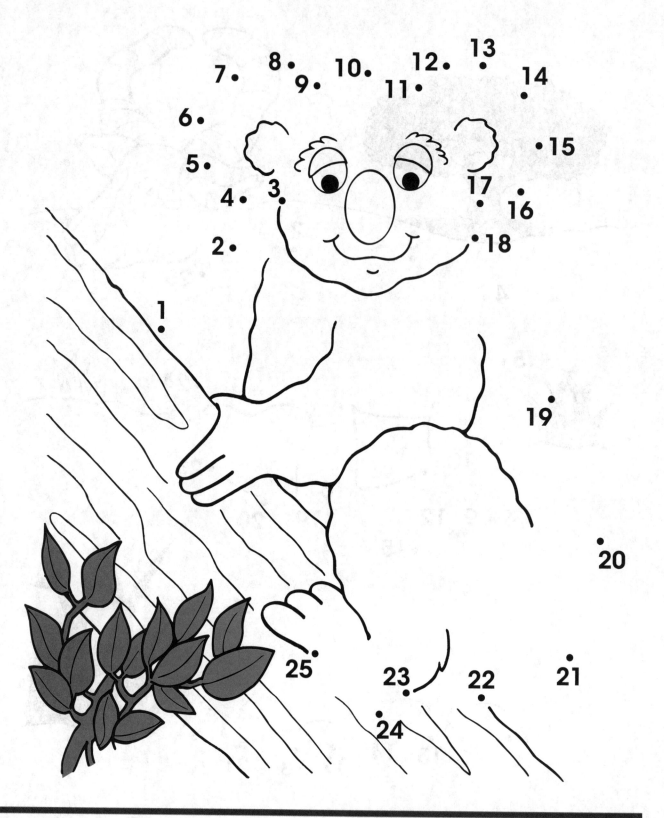

Bob Bighorn

Directions: Connect the dots from **1** to **25**. Then, color to finish the picture.

Off to Space!

Directions: Connect the dots from **1** to **25**. Then, color to finish the picture.

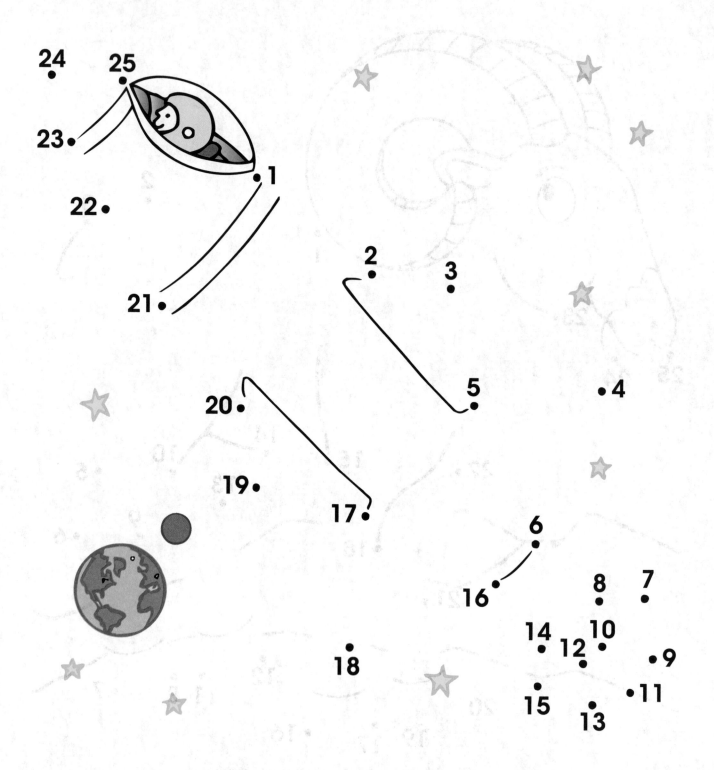

Leon Leopard

Directions: Connect the dots from **1** to **30**. Then, color to finish the picture.

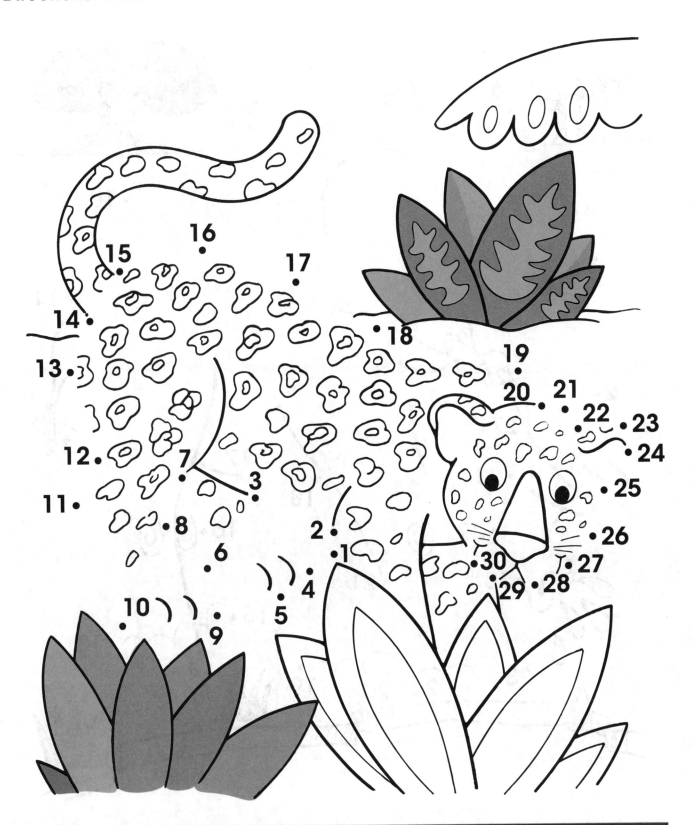

Erin Elephant

Directions: Connect the dots from **1** to **30**. Then, color to finish the picture.

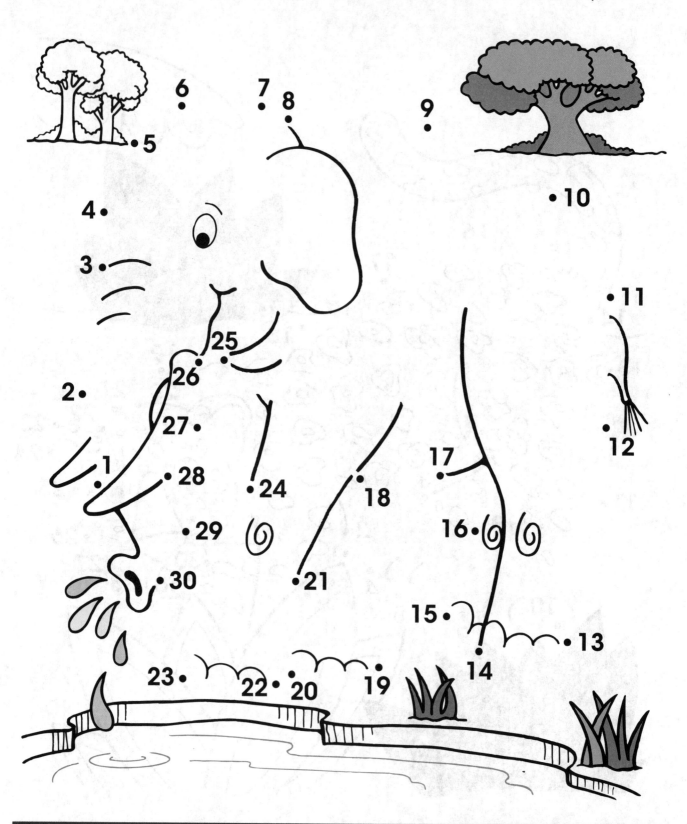

Tillie Tiger

Directions: Connect the dots from **1** to **30**. Then, color to finish the picture.

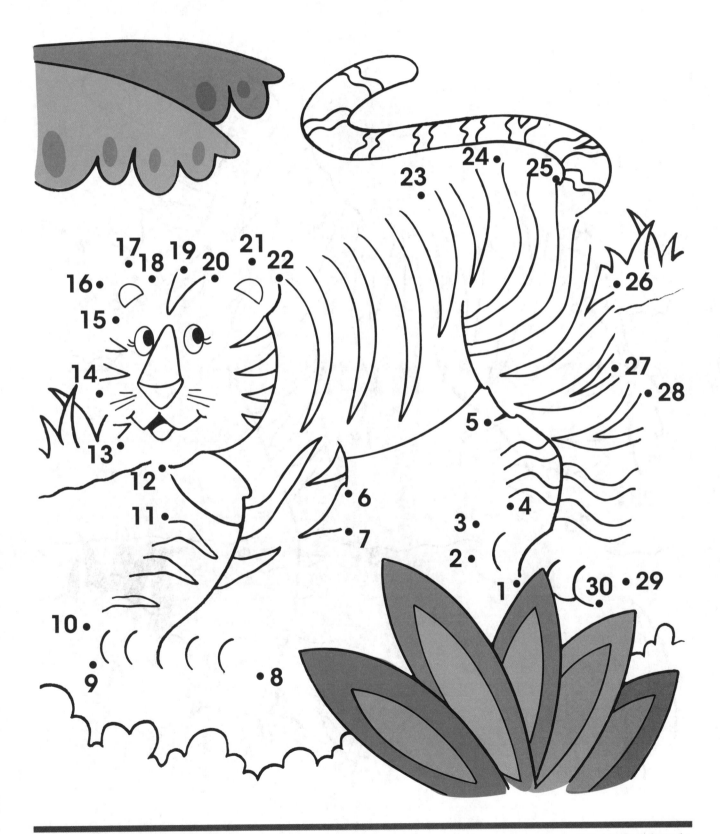

Zack Zebra

Directions: Connect the dots from **1** to **30**. Then, color to finish the picture.

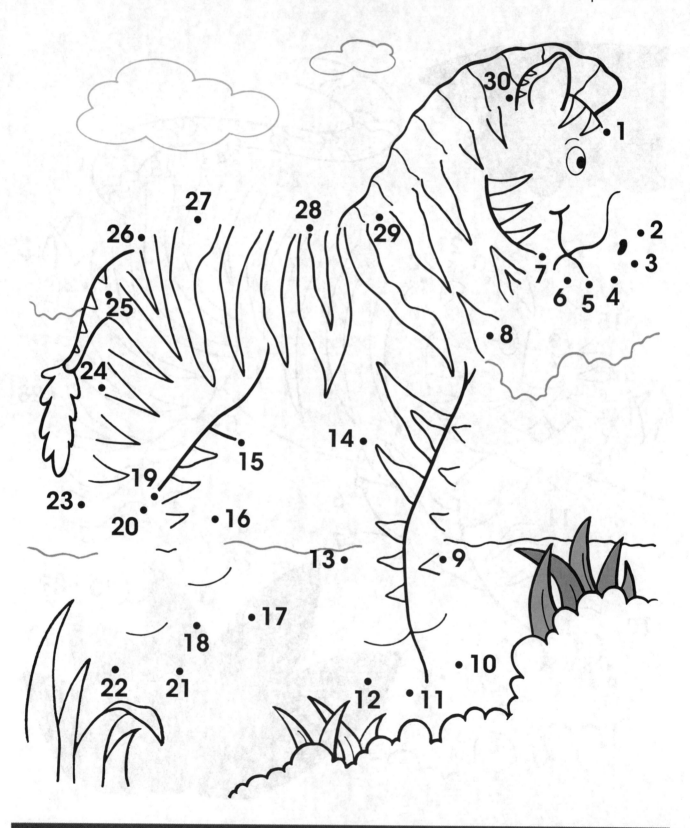

Mark Monkey

Directions: Connect the dots from **1** to **40**. Then, color to finish the picture.

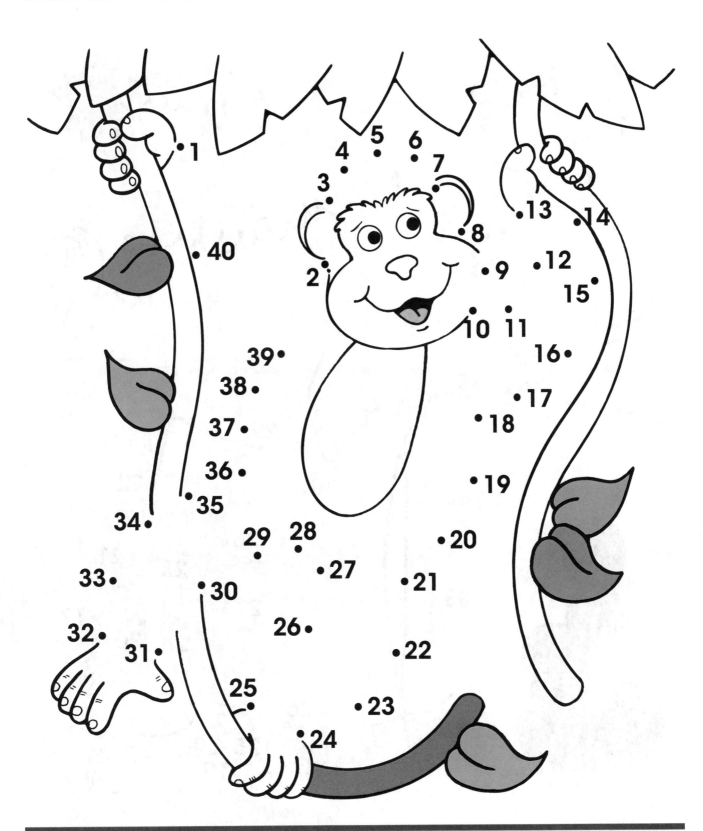

Carmen Camel

Directions: Connect the dots from **1** to **40**. Then, color to finish the picture.

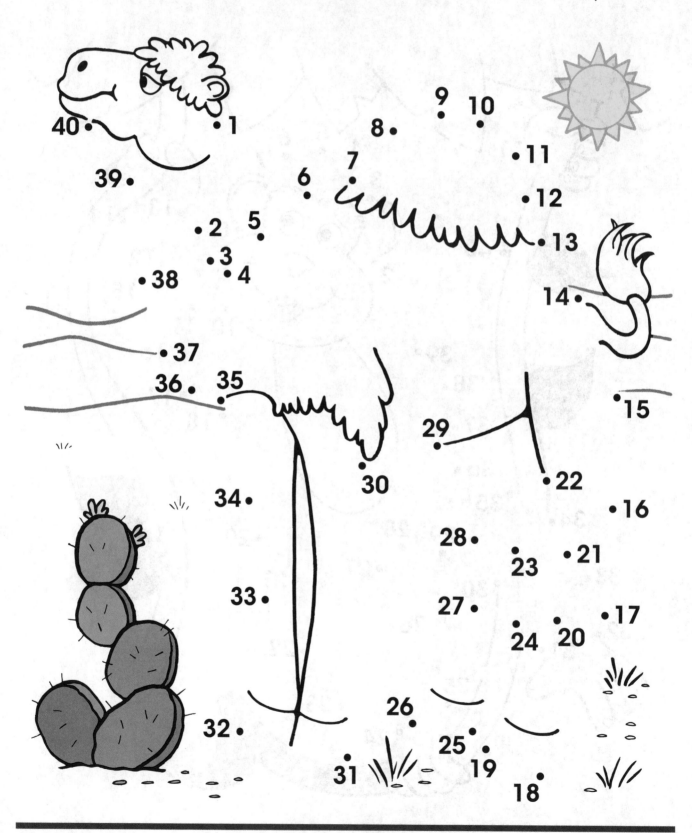

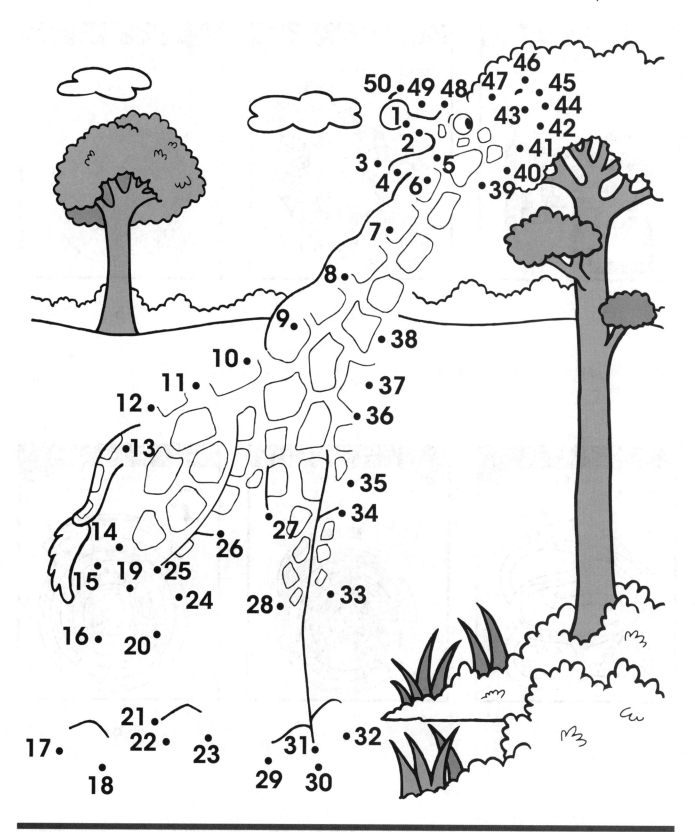

George Giraffe

Directions: Connect the dots from **1** to **50**. Then, color to finish the picture.

Answer Key

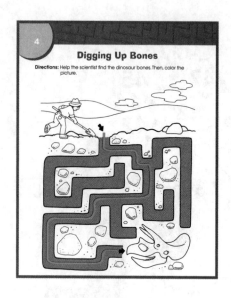

4

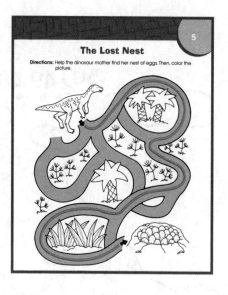

5

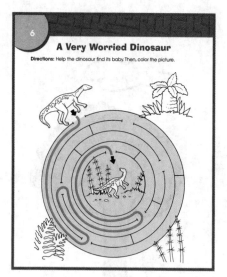

6

7

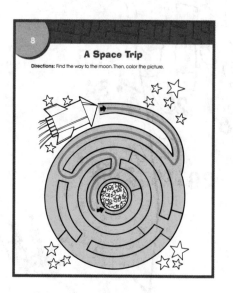

8

9

Answer Key

A Garden Helper

Directions: Find the way to the flower garden. Then, color the picture.

10

A Boat Ride

Directions: Follow the path to the island. Then, color the picture.

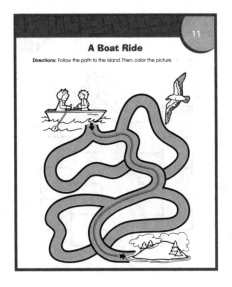

11

Forest Babies

Directions: Help the babies find their mothers. Then, color the picture.

12

Pinky's Bedtime

Directions: Find the way to Pinky's bed. Then, color the picture.

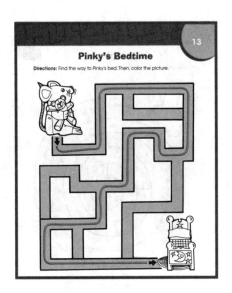

13

Time for Art

Directions: Help Anna find her drawing pad. Then, color the picture.

14

Soccer Fun

Directions: Help the soccer player score a goal. Then, color the picture.

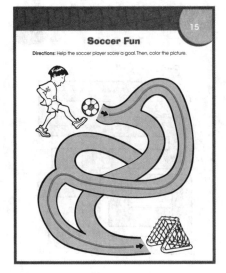

15

Answer Key

Bath Time

Directions: Help the boy get to the bathtub. Then, color the picture.

16

Bubble Gum

Directions: Help the girl find the gum. Then, color the picture.

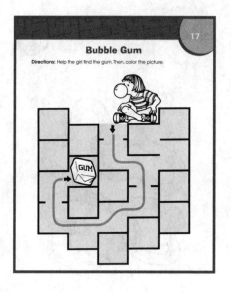

17

A Lost Shoe

Directions: Help the bug find its shoe. Then, color the picture.

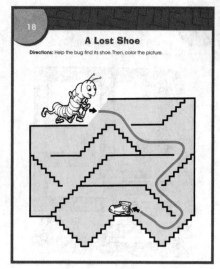

18

Time for Bed

Directions: Help the sleepy bear find the bed. Then, color the picture.

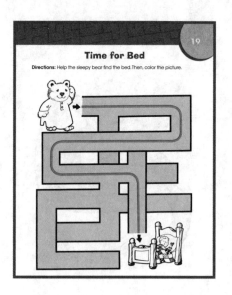

19

Busy Beaver

Directions: Help the beaver find the water. Then, color the picture.

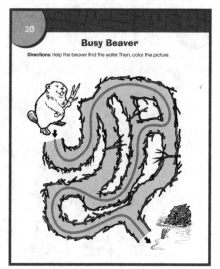

20

Springtime

Directions: Help the bunny find the egg. Then, color the picture.

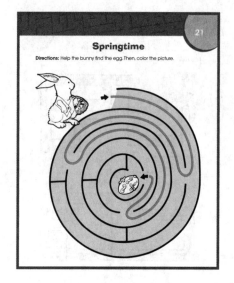

21

Answer Key

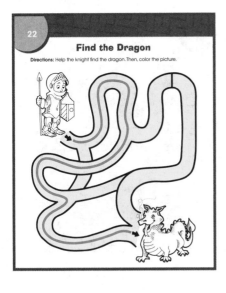

22

23

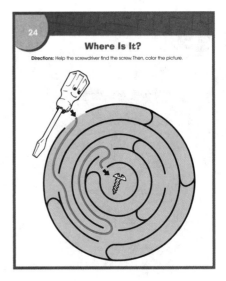

24

25

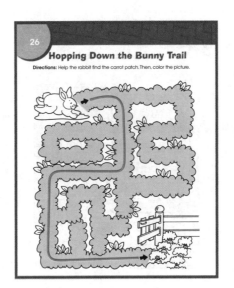

26

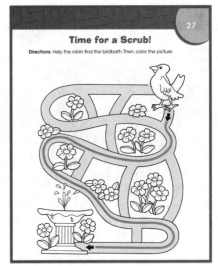

27

Answer Key

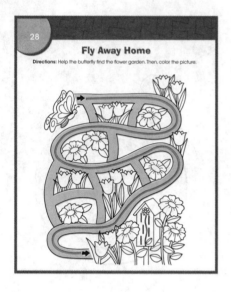

Fly Away Home
Directions: Help the butterfly find the flower garden. Then, color the picture.

28

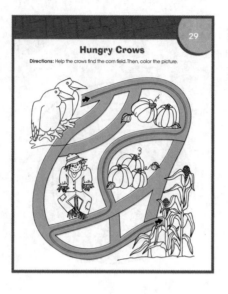

Hungry Crows
Directions: Help the crows find the corn field. Then, color the picture.

29

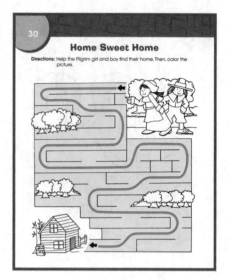

Home Sweet Home
Directions: Help the Pilgrim girl and boy find their home. Then, color the picture.

30

Little Lost Lamb
Directions: Help the lamb find its mother. Then, color the picture.

31

Let's Get to Work
Directions: Help the driver find the dump truck. Then, color the picture.

32

The New World
Directions: Help the Pilgrims find Plymouth Rock. Then, color the picture.

33

Answer Key

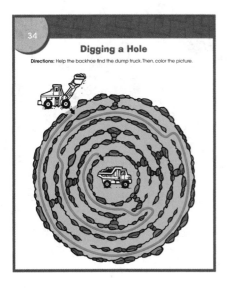

Digging a Hole

Directions: Help the backhoe find the dump truck. Then, color the picture.

34

Time for a Break

Directions: Help the foreman find the lunch truck. Then, color the picture.

35

Back from the Fire

Directions: Help the fire engine get to the fire station. Then, color the picture.

36

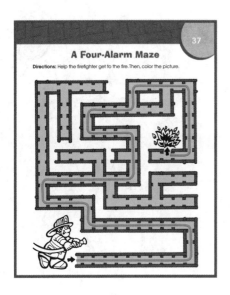

A Four-Alarm Maze

Directions: Help the firefighter get to the fire. Then, color the picture.

37

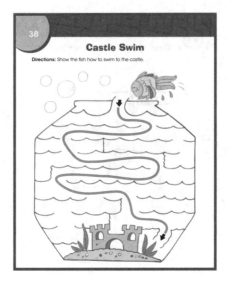

Castle Swim

Directions: Show the fish how to swim to the castle.

38

Keep the Beat

Directions: Connect the dots from **a** to **g**. Then, color to finish the picture.

39

Answer Key

40

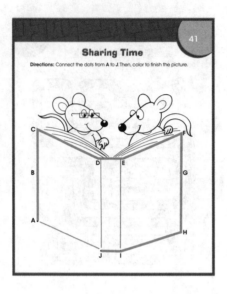

41

42

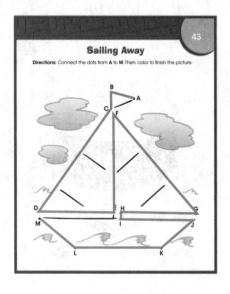

43

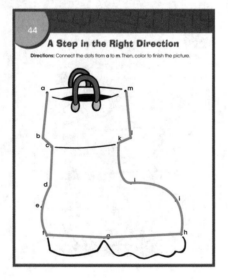

44

45

Answer Key

46

47

48

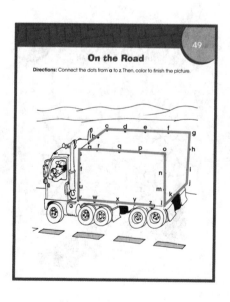

49

50

51

Answer Key

52

53

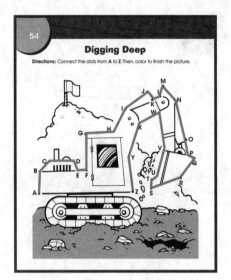

54

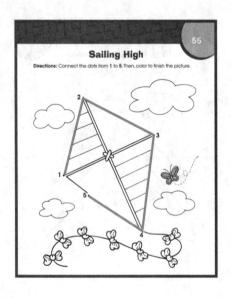

55

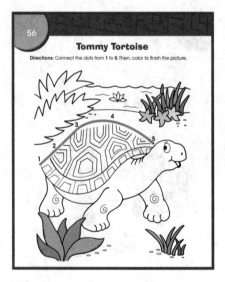

56

57

Answer Key

58

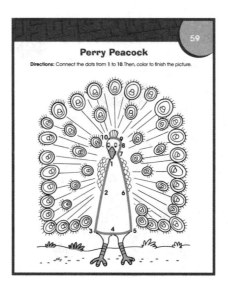

59

60

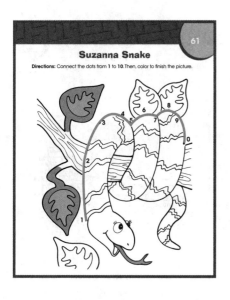

61

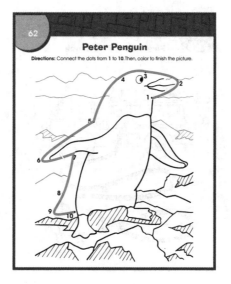

62

63

Answer Key

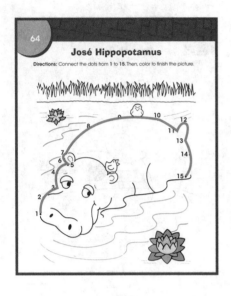

José Hippopotamus
Directions: Connect the dots from 1 to 15. Then, color to finish the picture.

64

Luke Llama
Directions: Connect the dots from 1 to 15. Then, color to finish the picture.

65

Pancho Polar Bear
Directions: Connect the dots from 1 to 15. Then, color to finish the picture.

66

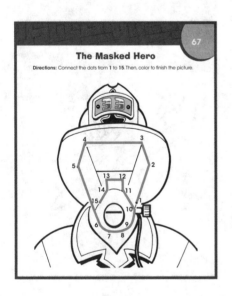

The Masked Hero
Directions: Connect the dots from 1 to 15. Then, color to finish the picture.

67

Fire Truck, Fire Truck
Directions: Connect the dots from 1 to 20. Then, color to finish the picture.

68

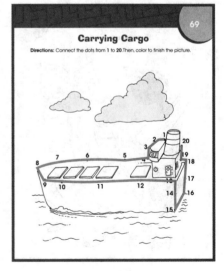

Carrying Cargo
Directions: Connect the dots from 1 to 20. Then, color to finish the picture.

69

Answer Key

70

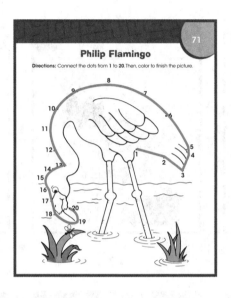

71

72

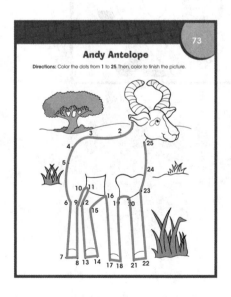

73

74

75

Answer Key

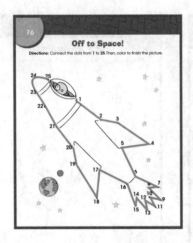

76

77

78

79

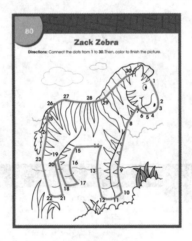

80

81

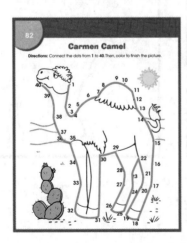

82

83